Writing Skills Builder

Level 4
English

Previously published as Success with Writing and Week-by-Week Homework for
Building Writing Skills Grades 3–5 by Scholastic Inc.

This edition published by Scholastic Education International (Singapore) Private Limited
A division of Scholastic Inc.

Scholastic Education International (Singapore) Private Limited
81 Ubi Avenue 4 #02-28 UB.ONE Singapore 408830
education@scholastic.com.sg

First edition 2013

ISBN 978-981-07-3282-0

Welcome to studySMART!

Writing Skills Builder provides opportunities for the systematic development of your child's writing skills as she progresses from word to sentence to paragraph.

It is often a challenge to help children develop their writing skills. The high-interest topics and engaging exercises in this book will both stimulate and encourage your child to develop the necessary skills to become an independent writer. As your child encounters a variety of texts and language features, she will learn to select the appropriate language structures and plan, write and proofread her writing.

Every section targets a specific skill and there are two mini-projects that are appropriately placed to ensure that your child uses the skills she has picked up in previous sections.

How to use this book?

1. Introduce the target writing skill at the top of the page to your child.

2. Direct her attention to the Note, where there is one, and go through the skills tip with your child.

3. Let your child complete the writing exercises.

4. Reinforce your child's learning with an extension activity at the end of each activity. These activities provide additional practice, and extend your child's learning of the particular writing skill.

Note: To avoid the awkward 'he or she' construction, the pronouns on this page and in the parents' notes will refer to the female gender.

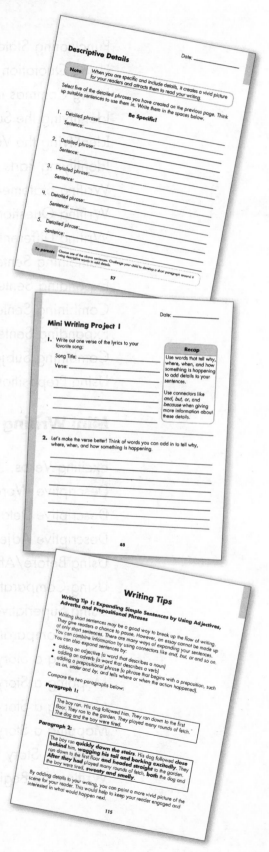

Contents

5

Punctuating Statements, Questions and Exclamations

Note	Every sentence begins with a capital letter. A statement ends with a period. A question ends with a question mark. An exclamation ends with an exclamation point.

Write each sentence correctly.

The Sunny Sahara

1. the Sahara Desert is in Africa

_____

2. do people live in the Sahara Desert

_____

3. the Sahara Desert is about the same size as the United States

_____

4. how high is the temperature in the Sahara Desert

_____

5. once the temperature reached 138°F

_____

To parents On another piece of paper, write a sentence with two mistakes. Ask your child to circle the mistakes.

Punctuating Statements, Questions and Exclamations

Write each sentence correctly.

Here Comes the Football Team!

1. the football team from Brooklyn School is here

   _____

2. they are playing against our school this evening

   _____

3. we are here at the stadium

   _____

4. are there any seats left at the grand stand

   _____

5. did you see the striker score a goal

   _____

6. what an exciting game

   _____

To parents On another piece of paper, ask your child to write three sentences about a game that she might have watched. Review the sentences and ensure that the correct punctuation has been used.

Punctuating Statements, Questions and Exclamations

Write out the story correctly.

A Secret!

one afternoon Sue was walking towards her class just then she saw Milly whispering to James

when they saw her they stopped and went back to their seats what was going on

on the 1st of July as Sue was entering her classroom she saw that all the windows were closed when she opened the door she heard a loud cheer Milly and James had planned a surprise party for her

_____

_____

_____

_____

_____

_____

_____

_____

To parents On another piece of paper, challenge your child to continue the story by adding a few more sentences to it. Review the sentences and ensure that the correct punctuation has been used.

Using Quotation Marks and Punctuation

Note	Quotation marks surround a character's exact words. In a statement, use a comma to separate the character's exact words from the rest of the sentence. In a question and an exclamation, use the correct ending punctuation after the character's exact words.

Statement: "I have to go now," said my friend.
Question: "Where are you?" asked my mom.
Exclamation: "Wow!" the boy exclaimed.

Write a sentence to match each speech bubble.

Look Who's Talking!

Somebody turned out the lights!

_____

_____

What makes you think I've been eating cookies?

_____

_____

My parents finally let me get my ears pierced.

_____

_____

To parents	On another piece of paper, ask your child to write a conversation she had with a friend during the day.

9

Using Quotation Marks and Punctuation

Note	Quotation marks surround a character's exact words, including the punctuation that comes with the sentence.

Read the story. Use the helping words to write conversation sentences and make the story more interesting. Remember to use commas when needed and the correct ending punctuation.

A Fine Day for Skateboarding

Larry picked up his skateboard and looked out the window. It was a bright and

sunny day. _____ he said to

himself happily. (fine day, skateboarding)

He went downstairs. Mom was making breakfast. Mom asked, _____

_____ (like, breakfast) Larry thought

for a while and said, "Pancakes, please!"

While he ate, Mom asked, "With whom will you be going skateboarding?"

Larry said _____

(Margie, Jensen)

Mom said _____ (home, six

o'clock, dinner) Larry said _____ (will)

To parents	On another piece of paper, challenge your child to write five sentences to continue the story and include at least one conversation sentence.

10

Using Quotation Marks and Punctuation

Cut out a favorite comic strip and paste it in the space here.
Write out what the characters are saying in the lines below.
Use the correct punctuation.

Comic Strip Title: _____

_____

_____

_____

_____

_____

_____

_____

_____

To parents   On a separate sheet of paper, ask your child to write a different set of conversation sentences for this comic strip. Remind her that she can use statements, questions and exclamations.

Using Commas in Sentences

| Note | Commas are used to separate items in a series of three or more. |

Write the sentences correctly using commas.

Listing It Out!

1. Betty has two pencils an eraser and a ruler in her pencil case.

    _____

2. Can I have a steak a salad and a glass of juice?

    _____

3. Aunt Nancy has been to Arkansas Colorado Florida and Michigan.

    _____

4. My sporty brother enjoys football basketball volleyball and hockey.

    _____

5. The three colors on the American flag are white red and blue.

    _____

6. Those trees are big tall and shady.

    _____

7. My father mother and elder sister are all at Uncle Jay's house.

    _____

8. I have Math History and Geography homework today.

    _____

| To parents | On another piece of paper, ask your child to write three more sentences, each with a series of three or more items. |

Using Commas in Sentences

Write the sentences correctly using commas.

Sunset

It was sunset. The sky was a mixture of red orange and purple. There were people strolling jogging and running. Some had their pet dogs with them. I could see terriers cocker spaniels beagles and golden retrievers. Harry Jack and Abby ran towards me. We love sunsets.

_____

_____

_____

_____

_____

Oh Deer!

The deer is a beautiful animal. It can hear well jump high swim fast and see in the dark. In the United States, there are mule deer white-tailed deer reindeer moose and elk. The mule deer lives in mountains canyon lands deserts and plains. The white-tailed deer feeds on leaves nuts berries and roots. The moose is the largest deer in the world. The elk is the second largest species in the country.

_____

_____

_____

_____

_____

To parents Ask your child to find out three interesting facts about her favorite animal. Then get her to write out a sentence that contains those facts.

Identifying the Subject of a Sentence

Note	A sentence tells about someone or something. This is called the **subject**.

Write the letter to show the subject of each sentence.

Sentences That Slither

A. The short blind snake
B. Tree snakes
C. The flowerpot snake
D. Bird snakes
E. A pit viper snake
F. All snakes

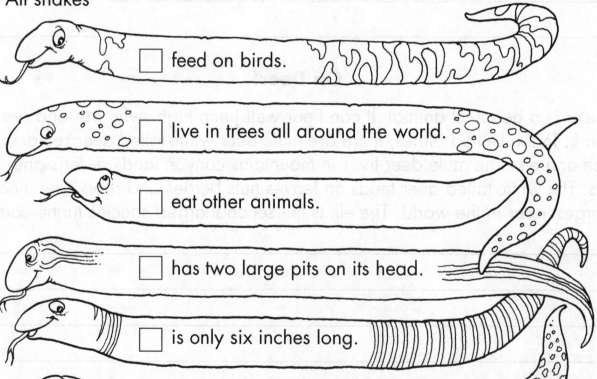

☐ feed on birds.

☐ live in trees all around the world.

☐ eat other animals.

☐ has two large pits on its head.

☐ is only six inches long.

☐ got its name from hiding in flowerpots.

To parents	Ask your child to write two sentences without the subject part. Then see if you can understand the sentences.

Identifying the Subject of a Sentence

Note	The subject of a sentence is the person, place, thing, or idea that the sentence is about.

Use the words given below to make sentences.
Circle the subject in each sentence you make.

A Day Out!

1. (radio, loud)

   _____

2. (sea, beautiful)

   _____

3. (burger, juicy, delicious)

   _____

4. (sun, shining)

   _____

5. (Mike, splashing)

   _____

6. (Michelle, cycling)

   _____

To parents	Read a short article in a magazine or the newspaper. Ask your child to circle all the subjects she can find in it.

Identifying the Subject of a Sentence

Write down the subjects you circled on the previous page. Write out new sentences about these subjects.

1. Subject: _____

    _____

    _____

2. Subject: _____

    _____

    _____

3. Subject: _____

    _____

    _____

4. Subject: _____

    _____

    _____

5. Subject: _____

    _____

    _____

6. Subject: _____

    _____

    _____

To parents On a separate sheet of paper, ask your child to write down three subjects she can see. They can be people, places or things. Then ask your child to make a sentence about each with them.

Identifying the Verb of a Sentence

| **Note** | A sentence tells what the subject does or is. This part of the sentence is called the **verb**. |

Use the list of subjects as the beginning for eight sentences. Then add a verb to tell what the subject is doing.

A Reptile Fact Sheet

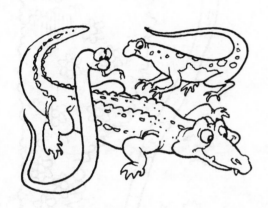

Snake
Lizard
Crocodile
Turtle
Dinosaur
Iguana
Alligator
Python

1. _____
2. _____
3. _____
4. _____
5. _____
6. _____
7. _____
8. _____

| **To parents** | On another piece of paper, ask your child to write three sentences about what she likes to do after school. Have your child circle the verb in each sentence. |

Identifying the Verb of a Sentence

> **Note** The verb of a sentence tells us what the subject is or is doing.

Underline the verb(s) in each of these sentences.

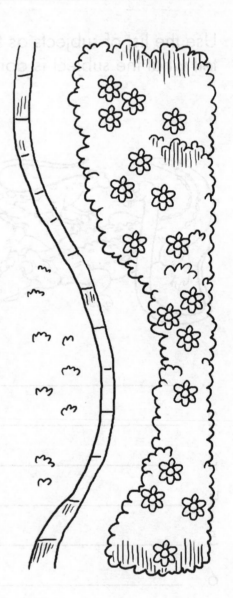

1. My mother loves flowers.

2. Every day, she waters the flowers.

3. She also puts fertilizer.

4. She pulls out the weeds and prunes the plant.

5. The flowers bloom beautifully.

6. I like flowers too.

7. Sometimes, I help my mother with the flowers.

8. Sometimes, we pluck the flowers.

9. We place the flowers in a vase.

10. The room looks fresh when there are flowers.

To parents Pick out a paragraph from a chapter in a storybook. Ask your child to rewrite the paragraph using more interesting verbs.

Identifying the Verb of a Sentence

Rewrite the story in the past tense by changing the underlined verbs.

A Trip to the Zoo

Jan <u>is</u> going to the zoo. She <u>is</u> very excited. Her mother <u>packs</u> a sandwich and a bottle of milk into her bag. Her mother <u>says</u>, "Listen to Miss Davis and do not run about." Jan <u>replies</u>, "Yes, mom. Can I go now?" Jan's mother <u>smiles</u> and <u>waves</u> as Jan <u>skips</u> towards the school bus.

_____

_____

_____

_____

Rewrite the next part of the story in the past tense by yourself.

At the zoo, she sees many animals. There are the regal lions, the graceful giraffes, and the playful monkeys. Soon it is time for lunch. Jan sits with her friends and unwraps her sandwich. "Oh, it's my favorite cheese sandwich!" she exclaims.

_____

_____

_____

_____

_____

To parents Ask your child to rewrite part of an article from a magazine by changing its verb to another form (from past tense to present tense or vice versa). Then ask her if the paragraph still makes sense.

Identifying Parts of a Sentence

| Note | A sentence needs two parts, a subject and a predicate, to express a complete thought.
The **subject part** tells whom or what the sentence is about.
The **predicate part** tells what the subject is or does. |

Birds of a feather
subject part

flock together.
predicate part

Link It Together

A. Read the subject and predicate parts from some other famous sayings. Write S next to each subject part. Write P next to each predicate part.

_____ spoils the whole barrel   _____ has a silver lining

_____ every cloud   _____ makes waste

_____ catches the worm   _____ one rotten apple

_____ the early bird   _____ a rolling stone

_____ gathers no moss   _____ haste

B. Now combine the subject and predicate parts to create these famous sayings.

1. _____

2. _____

3. _____

4. _____

5. _____

| To parents | Make up some sayings with your child. Then ask her to circle the subject part and underline the predicate part of each sentence. |

Writing Statements

| **Note** | A statement is used to answer a question. |

Use a complete sentence to write the answer to each question.

Rock and Roll

1. How many types of rocks are on our planet? (three)

    _____

2. How hot is the melted rock inside the earth? (more than 2000°F)

    _____

3. Where are most igneous rocks formed? (inside the earth)

    _____

4. What type of rock is marble? (metamorphic)

    _____

5. In what type of rock are fossils found? (sedimentary)

    _____

| **To parents** | Ask your child a question and get her to answer in a complete sentence. |

Writing Statements

Note	A statement begins with a capital letter and ends with a period.

Look at the poster and use a complete sentence to answer each question.

The Circus Is Coming to Town!

1. What is the name of the circus? (Barker and Barnes)

    _____

2. Which state will the circus be visiting? (Kansas)

    _____

3. When will the circus be performing? (19–24 May)

    _____

4. What are the show times? (4.30 pm and 8.00 pm)

    _____

To parents	On a separate sheet of paper, write another question about the circus and ask your child to answer the question using a complete sentence.

Writing Statements

Read the advertisement. Use a complete sentence to answer each question.

Mega Sale!

THE ANNUAL MEGA SPORTS SALE!!

14 July - 17 July 2012
National Auditorium,
7 Boulevard Road

More than 500 deals on sportswear, equipment and accessories!!

1. What is the name of the sale?

   _____

2. How many deals are there at the sale?

   _____

3. When will the sale start?

   _____

4. How many days will the sale last?

   _____

To parents Look out for another advertisement in the newspaper. Write a few questions about the advertisement and ask your child to answer the questions using complete sentences.

Writing Statements

Note	A question begins with a capital letter and ends with a question mark (**?**). It often begins with one of the words listed below.

Who	When
Will	Can
What	Why
Would	Did
Where	How
Should	Is

Imagine that you are interviewing your favorite famous person. Write five questions you would ask this person. Use a different beginning word for each question.

The Real World

I am interviewing _____

1. _____

2. _____

3. _____

4. _____

5. _____

To parents On another piece of paper, ask your child to write an answer to each question.

Writing Questions

Write questions to fit the answer sentences.

Life of the Party!

1. _____ (Why)

They are laughing because Tom just told a joke.

2. _____ (Should)

Yes, you should bring out the cake now.

3. _____ (Did)

No, Pat did not come to the party today.

4. _____ (When)

His parents are coming back at 11 o'clock tonight.

5. _____ (Where)

The glasses are in the glass cabinet.

6. _____ (Can)

Yes, Ivan can have some chocolate ice cream.

7. _____ (Will)

Yes, we will be playing games.

8. _____ (What)

Let's play "Pirates and Sailors"!

> **To parents** Write down three statements. Ask your child to write three questions that fit the statements.

Writing Questions

Mrs Talky is on the phone with Mr Talky. Try to guess the questions that Mr Talky is asking Mrs Talky. Write them down in the spaces below.

What Did He Say?

Mr Talky: _____

Mrs Talky: Oh, I was just putting the chicken into the oven when you called.

Mr Talky: _____

Mrs Talky: Our neighbors, Mr and Mrs Moore, will be coming to dinner tonight.

Mr Talky: _____

Mrs Talky: Yes, they will be bringing their children along.

Mr Talky: _____

Mrs Talky: Oh, everything is going just fine.

Mr Talky: _____

Mrs Talky: Please be back home by eight o'clock.

To parents Ask your child to listen to one of your family members when they next talk on the phone. Then, ask your child to write down three possible questions that the person on the other end might be asking.

Writing Different Types of Sentences

Read the topics below and then write four different types of sentences that might tell about each topic. Be sure to use a capital letter at the beginning of each sentence and the correct punctuation. Here is an example to get you started:

Topic: You are going swimming.

    Statement: I am putting on my new swimsuit.

    Question: Do you have a new suit, too?

    Exclamation: What a great color!

    Command: Jump in, the water's great!

Topic: You have a substitute teacher today.

    Statement: _____

    Question: _____

    Exclamation: _____

    Command: _____

Topic: It is your birthday.

    Statement: _____

    Question: _____

    Exclamation: _____

    Command: _____

Topic: There will be no school tomorrow because of bad weather.

Statement: _____

Question: _____

Exclamation: _____

Command: _____

Topic: Your team just won the country championship.

Statement: _____

Question: _____

Exclamation: _____

Command: _____

Topic: Your dog just ate your hamburger.

Statement: _____

Question: _____

Exclamation: _____

Command: _____

Date: _____

Writing Different Types of Sentences

Write different types of sentences using the words given. You may use the words in any order.

Example: answer, question
Statement: I have the answer to the question.
Exclamation: I have the answer to the question!
Question: Do you have the answer to the question?
Command: Answer the question!

1. open, door

   Statement: _____

   Exclamation: _____

   Question: _____

   Command: _____

2. boat, faster

   Statement: _____

   Exclamation: _____

   Question: _____

   Command: _____

To parents | Select a statement from a favorite storybook. Ask your child to rewrite it as an exclamation, a question and a command.

Writing Different Types of Sentences

Write sentences to tell more about the situations given. Include at least one of each type of sentence – statement, exclamation, question and command.

A Puppy for Me!

Your father has just bought you a puppy, a pet that you have always wanted.

Father: Surprise! Look what I've got you!

You: _____

Father: _____

You: _____

Father: _____

You: _____

What an Exciting Match!

Tom is watching a basketball tournament with his friend, Ben. Both boys are following the game excitedly.

Tom: _____

Ben: _____

Tom: _____

Ben: _____

Tom: _____

Ben: _____

To parents Ask your child to add two more lines of conversation to each of the above conversation threads.

Writing Different Types of Sentences

You are the scriptwriter of the movie "The Treasure Hunt". Write out the scene using statements, exclamations, questions and commands.

The Treasure Hunt

Scene: The characters have found a treasure map and are deciding what to do next.

Characters:
Ray – An adventurous boy. He is the one who found the map.
Jason – Ray's best friend
Maggie – Ray's younger sister. She is very good at reading maps.

Ray   : Hey, look what I found! It's a treasure map!

_____ : _____

_____

_____ : _____

_____

_____ : _____

_____

_____ : _____

_____

_____ : _____

_____

To parents   Think of the next scene. Ask your child to write five conversation sentences for it. Include at least one statement, exclamation, question and command.

Combining Sentences

Note	Sentences can also be combined to make them more interesting. Key words can help put two sentences together. For example: I will plan my garden. I am waiting for spring. I will plan my garden **while** I am waiting for spring.

Combine the two sentences using the given key word. Write a new sentence.

Great Gardening Tips

1. Fill a cup with water. Add some flower seeds.

_____

2. This will soften the seeds. They are hard.

_____

3. Fill a cup with dirt. The seeds soak in water.

_____

4. Bury the seeds in the cup. The dirt covers them.

_____

5. Add water to the plant. Do not add too much.

_____

6. Set the cup in the sun. The plant will grow.

_____

Combining Sentences

Note	Sentences can be combined to make them more interesting.

Write a combined sentence of your own. Use the given key word to help you.
The first one has been done for you.

Growing Sentences

1. while: <u>I watch TV while my mom makes lunch.</u>

2. until: _____

   _____

3. because: _____

   _____

4. but: _____

   _____

5. or: _____

   _____

6. and: _____

   _____

To parents	On another piece of paper, ask your child to write a combined sentence using one of the key words: 'after', 'before' or 'during'.

Expanding Sentences

Note	A sentence is more interesting when it includes more than just a subject and a verb. It may tell where, when, or why something is happening.

Write a sentence describing each set of pictures. Include a part that tells where, when, or why something is happening.

Stretching Sentences

1. _____

2. _____

3. _____

4. _____

To parents	Find a cartoon strip in the newspaper. Use the pictures and ask your child to write a sentence on another piece of paper that includes a subject, a verb, and a part that tells where, when, or why.

Expanding Sentences

Make the sentences more interesting by including the words in the brackets.

Example: James looks pale. (unwell)
James looks pale because he is unwell.

Stretching More Sentences

1. Rita keeps her toys in the cabinet. (dirty)

_____

2. I will meet Brenda. (five in the evening)

_____

3. They are going for dinner. (restaurant down the street)

_____

4. Trey and Johnson are playing ball. (basketball court)

_____

5. My family is going for a holiday. (December)

_____

6. It is a good time to go out to play. (weather is fine)

_____

7. Aunt Kathy will be visiting us. (her meeting)

_____

To parents   Write a simple sentence on a separate sheet of paper. Ask your child to add more details about where, when, or why to make the sentence more interesting.

Expanding Sentences

Look at the pictures and read the story. Make it more interesting by adding the helping words to each part of the story.

Ali Baba and the Forty Thieves

1. Ali Baba, a woodcutter, saw forty thieves. The leader said "Open Sesame!" and the mouth of the cave opened. The thieves went in.

   | afternoon | cave | forest | magically | quickly |

   _____

   _____

2. Ali Baba hid outside the cave entrance and peeped in. He saw the thieves putting their treasures in the cave. He saw a lot of treasures.

   | could not see | beautiful | on the floor |

   _____

   _____

3. Ali Baba told his brother about the cave. His brother decided to visit the cave. In the night, he went out.

   | amazing cave | that night | everyone was asleep |

   _____

   _____

To parents Challenge your child to continue the story using words to tell where, when, why, and how the next events are happening.

Combining Sentences with Conjunctions

| **Note** | Two sentences can be combined to make one sentence by using the words *although, after, because, until* and *while*. |

Choose a word from the menu to combine the two sentences into one sentence.

Let's Eat Out!

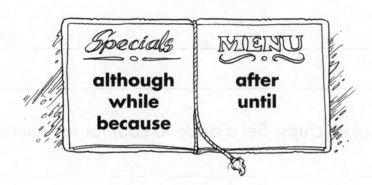

1. We are eating out tonight. Mom worked late.

   _____

2. We are going to Joe's Fish Shack. I do not like fish.

   _____

3. Dad said I can play outside. It's time to leave.

   _____

4. We can play video games. We are waiting for our food.

   _____

5. We may stop by Ida's Ice Cream Shop. We leave the restaurant.

   _____

| **To parents** | Read the back of a cereal box. Ask your child to find two sentences that could be combined. |

Date: _____

Combining Sentences with Conjunctions

Read the recipe. Combine steps in the instructions using *although*, *after*, *because*, *until* and *while*.

Homemade ChocoNuts Recipe!

1. Cook sugar and water in a saucepan. The sugar has melted.

   _____

   _____

2. Stir in the chocolate chips. Set it aside to cool for ten minutes.

   _____

   _____

3. The chocolate mixture is cooling. Pour the nuts into the mixture.

   _____

   _____

4. Place the mixture into the refrigerator. That will harden it quickly.

   _____

   _____

5. This recipe uses nuts. You can use dried fruits instead.

   _____

   _____

Expanding Sentences with Descriptive Words

Note	A **describing word** makes a sentence more interesting.

At the Beach

Read the describing words found in the beach balls. Add the describing words to make each sentence more interesting. Write each new sentence.

1. The snow cone sat in the sun.

   _____

2. Many children ran toward the ocean waves.

   _____

3. My friends built a sandcastle.

   _____

4. My brother grabbed his beach toys.

   _____

5. Our dog tried to catch the beach balls.

   _____

To parents	On another piece of paper, draw a beach ball. Ask your child to fill it with words that describe a day at the beach.

Expanding Sentences with Descriptive Words

| Note | A **describing word** can tell more about a subject or a verb. |

Add describing words to make each sentence more interesting.

The Great Outdoors

1. The _____ hikers walked back to camp _____.

2. The _____ bird sang _____.

3. The _____ tree grew _____.

4. The _____ children played _____.

5. My _____ sister swam _____.

6. The _____ crickets chirped _____.

7. The _____ flowers bloomed _____.

8. The _____ swing set creaked _____.

9. The _____ ice cream melted _____.

10. The _____ trees shook _____ in the storm.

| To parents | On another piece of paper, ask your child to write the name of her favorite outdoor place. Then write three words that describe it. |

Expanding Sentences with Descriptive Words

Add describing words to make the story more detailed and interesting.

Lost and Found!

One _____ morning, Kevin was walking along a

_____ sidewalk when he caught sight of a _____

wallet on the ground. He picked it up and found a _____ piece

of paper inside. He was surprised to find Aunt Mary's name and old address on it.

Just then, a _____ old man walked towards him. "Ah! You found

my wallet." said the _____ man. Kevin said, "Here you go, sir.

How is it you know my Aunt Mary?" The old man gasped and said, "Mary is

your aunt? Why, I've been looking for that _____ friend of mine!

We've lost touch since we left school."

Kevin smiled and said, "She lives at the next street. Shall I take you there?" With

_____ hands, the old man grasped Kevin's hands and said,

"Thank you so much, young man!"

Combining Subjects, Predicates and Objects

Note	When two sentences have different subjects and the same predicate, you can combine them into one sentence with a compound subject using *and*.
	My friends ordered a pizza. I ordered a pizza.
	My friends and I ordered a pepperoni pizza.
	When two sentences have the same subject and different predicates, you can use *and* to combine them into one sentence with a compound predicate.
	My mom ordered. She had pasta instead.
	My mom ordered and had pasta instead.
	When two sentences have the same subject and predicate and different objects, you can combine them into one sentence with a compound object using *and*.
	My dad wanted anchovies on his pizza. He also wanted onions.
	My dad wanted anchovies and onions on his pizza.

Fill in the missing subject, object, or predicate in each set of shorter sentences. Then combine the sentences by making compound subjects, objects, or predicates using *and*.

Order the Combination

1. _____ are sweet and juicy.

   _____ are sweet and juicy.

   _____

2. I _____ about the history of basketball for homework.

   I _____ about the history of basketball for homework.

   _____

3. I like _____ more than broccoli or cauliflower.

   I like _____ more than broccoli or cauliflower.

   _____

Combine the sentences by making compound subjects, predicates, or objects using *and*.

1. Rene likes to eat stewed tomatoes.
   Rene likes to eat mashed potatoes.

   _____

   _____

2. Audrey will go to Holland next month.
   Candace will go to Holland next month.

   _____

   _____

3. I prefer reading adventure stories to biographies or non-fiction.
   I prefer reading horror stories to biographies or non-fiction.

   _____

   _____

4. Our market sells delicious local strawberries.
   Our market sells delicious imported strawberries.

   _____

   _____

5. Alexander Graham Bell was a scientist.
   Alexander Graham Bell was the inventor of the telephone.

   _____

   _____

Combining Subjects, Predicates and Objects

Combine the sentences in the story by making compound subjects, predicates or objects using *and*.

Marty and the Squirrel

It was a warm afternoon. It was a quiet afternoon. Marty the cat was lazing in the sun. Marty the cat was feeling sleepy.

Suddenly, Marty saw a movement in the bushes. Marty also saw the flash of a furry tail. He sat up. He pricked his ears.

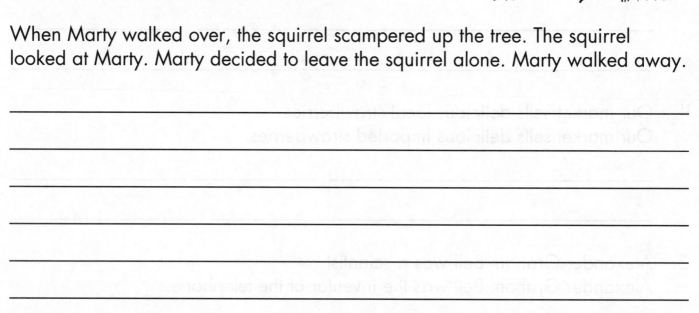

In the bushes was a busy squirrel. In the bushes was a hardworking squirrel. The squirrel was gathering acorns on the ground. The squirrel was also gathering acorns in the trees.

When Marty walked over, the squirrel scampered up the tree. The squirrel looked at Marty. Marty decided to leave the squirrel alone. Marty walked away.

_____

_____

_____

_____

_____

_____

_____

To parents Challenge your child to look up some information about an animal. Get her to write the information down on a separate sheet of paper and combine similar ideas together in sentences.

Using Prepositions to Write Extended Sentences

Note | Prepositions tell where something is.

Use the prepositions provided to add more details to the sentences.

Building with Prepositions

1. Jonathan sits down.

    On: _____

    Between: _____

    Across: _____

2. Irin walked slowly.

    Along: _____

    In: _____

    From: _____

3. Mandy looked carefully.

    At: _____

    Through: _____

    For: _____

4. We did not see her.

    After: _____

    Outside: _____

    Under: _____

To parents | Choose an object that you see around you. Ask your child to make three different sentences with it using three different prepositions.

45

Using Prepositions to Write Extended Sentences

Use suitable prepositions and the words in brackets to make the sentences more detailed.

Where and When?

1. He put the cup of coffee down. (table)

    _____

2. The hunter walked silently. (jungle)

    _____

3. There are many ripe apples. (apple tree)

    _____

4. Mr Johnson bumped into his neighbor. (corner)

    _____

5. People flock to the malls. (Christmas season)

    _____

6. She was listening to the radio. (washed the dishes)

    _____

7. Please brush your teeth. (go to bed)

    _____

8. The seagulls were flying. (sea)

    _____

To parents Together with your child, look at a picture in a storybook or a magazine. Focus on an item in the picture and ask your child to describe it using prepositions.

Using Prepositions to Write Extended Sentences

Look at the pictures. Using suitable prepositions and the words in the brackets, add more details to make the story more interesting.

Searching for Cheese

Once there were four mice. Every day they would look for cheese

_____ (mouse hole). They searched high and low,

_____ (table), _____

(chair) and _____ (kitchen).

One day, they found some cheese! It was wrapped up _____ (paper)

and kept _____ (refrigerator).

Whenever they could, they would gather the bits that had dropped

_____ (floor). Then, they would quickly scurry

_____ (room) back into their cozy home.

Mini Writing Project 1

1. Write out one verse of the lyrics to your favorite song:

Song Title: _____

Verse: _____

_____

_____

_____

_____

_____

Recap
Use words that tell why, where, when, and how something is happening to add details to your sentences. Use connectors like *and*, *but*, *or*, and *because* when giving more information about these details.

2. Let's make the verse better! Think of words you can add in to tell why, where, when, and how something is happening.

_____

_____

_____

_____

_____

_____

_____

3. Combine lines of lyrics from the verse together using connectors. Here are some examples of connectors:

and	but	or	because
although	however	unless	so

_____

_____

_____

_____

_____

_____

_____

_____

_____

_____

4. Check your sentences for mistakes.

Exciting Verbs

| Note | You can make your writing more interesting by using vivid verbs and using a variety of verbs. |

Under each verb write four livelier verbs that have the same or almost the same meaning.

Give it Life!

run	eat	write	make
1. _____	1. _____	1. _____	1. _____
2. _____	2. _____	2. _____	2. _____
3. _____	3. _____	3. _____	3. _____
4. _____	4. _____	4. _____	4. _____

move	speak	hit	look
1. _____	1. _____	1. _____	1. _____
2. _____	2. _____	2. _____	2. _____
3. _____	3. _____	3. _____	3. _____
4. _____	4. _____	4. _____	4. _____

Exciting Verbs

Replace the verbs in bold with livelier, more precise ones.

1. Michael **rode** his bicycle into a tree.

   _____

2. The pirate **got off** his ship and **went** into the water.

   _____

3. When the teacher **saw** that the girls were chewing gum, she **went** across the room to **talk to** them.

   _____

   _____

4. The entire football team **went** onto the field when they won the championship.

   _____

5. Emily **cut** open the contest envelope to see if she had won a prize.

   _____

6. All of a sudden the computer **moved** across the desk.

   _____

7. The cat **walked** across the top of the couch, **looking** down at the dog below.

   _____

To parents   Get your child to write down the list of verbs in a notebook and use that for future reference.

Exciting Verbs

Note	Different verbs may mean the same thing, but they can change the mood and tone of the sentences in which they are used. You may use a thesaurus to help you find replacement verbs.

Rewrite the sentence and replace the verbs in bold with livelier and more precise ones.

1. Mike fell from his bicycle and **cried** in pain.

    _____

2. Sarah was so hungry that she **ate** her lunch hurriedly.

    _____

    _____

3. As Peter **ran** to the toilet, he **ran** into his friend Jim.

    _____

    _____

4. Tania **opened** her present and **shouted** when she saw a pretty dress.

    _____

    _____

5. I **jumped** out from behind the wall and my brother **shouted**.

    _____

    _____

6. The kitten **looked** at the ball of wool and tried to **take** it with its paws.

    _____

    _____

To parents	Take a candid photograph of a family member. Ask your child to use suitable verbs to describe what he or she was doing.

Exciting Verbs

Pick out suitable verbs from the boxes to replace the words in bold in the sentences.

1. Janice was **walking slowly** in the park and **looking at** the scenery.

   | strolling | scampering | enjoying | examining |

   _____

   _____

2. Suddenly, she **saw** someone **looking steadily** at her from the bench.

   | noticed | observed | glancing | gazing |

   _____

   _____

3. When she **went closer** to him, she **saw** that it was Jon, her childhood friend.

   | approached | surrounded | spotted | realized |

   _____

   _____

4. Jon **smiled** and they sat down to **talk** happily.

   | guffawed | grinned | chat | whisper |

   _____

   _____

To parents   Ask your child to think of more verbs that can be used to describe actions. Make a list of these verbs for future reference.

Descriptive Words

Note	A **describing word** helps you imagine how something looks, feels, smells, sounds, or tastes.

Write a list of describing words on each bucket to fit the bucket's category.

Buckets of Fun

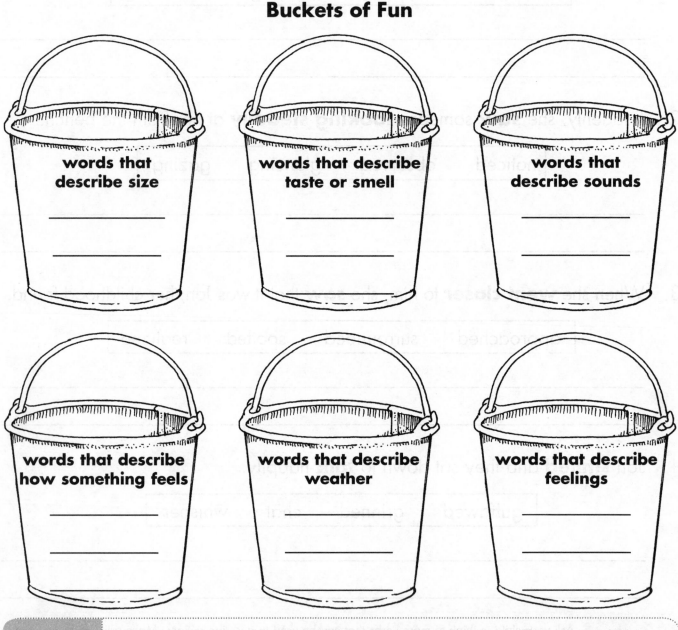

words that
describe size

words that describe
taste or smell

words that
describe sounds

words that describe
how something feels

words that describe
weather

words that describe
feelings

To parents	Ask your child to make a "mystery bag" by putting a secret object inside. Then get your child to describe the object to you so that you can guess what it is.

Descriptive Words

Note	A **describing word** can be added to a sentence. She wore a $_\wedge$ dress. `red`

Read the sentences about each picture. Then use the $\wedge$ mark as shown above to add a describing word to each sentence.

Outdoor Excitement

1. The girl picked flowers.

2. The girl swatted the bees.

3. A bee stung the girl.

1. The boy played a game.

2. The boy won a trophy.

3. The boy held his trophy.

To parents Ask your child to add two describing words to this sentence: The campers heard a sound in the night.

Date: _____

Descriptive Details

For each general word or phrase, write a more specific word. Then add details to describe each specific word.

Spout Some Specifics

	Specific Word	Details
1. a body of water	_____	_____
2. a piece of furniture	_____	_____
3. an article of clothing	_____	_____
4. a tool	_____	_____
5. a group of people	_____	_____
6. a reptile	_____	_____
7. a kind of fruit	_____	_____
8. a drink	_____	_____
9. a type of footwear	_____	_____
10. a musical instrument	_____	_____

To parents Ask your child to write words and phrases to describe herself so that someone who does not know her would get a clear, vivid picture of what she looks like.

Descriptive Details

Note	When you are specific and include details, it creates a vivid picture for your readers and attracts them to read your writing.

Select five of the detailed phrases you have created on the previous page. Think up suitable sentences to use them in. Write them in the spaces below.

Be Specific!

1. Detailed phrase:_____

   Sentence: _____

   _____

2. Detailed phrase:_____

   Sentence: _____

   _____

3. Detailed phrase:_____

   Sentence: _____

   _____

4. Detailed phrase:_____

   Sentence: _____

   _____

5. Detailed phrase:_____

   Sentence: _____

   _____

To parents	Choose one of the above sentences. Challenge your child to develop a short paragraph around it using descriptive words to add details.

Descriptive Details

Read the story below. Rewrite the story by adding your own details to the underlined nouns to create a better picture for your readers.

The Foolish Man and His Donkey

One day, a <u>man</u> said to his <u>son</u>, "Let's go to the market and sell our <u>donkey</u>." So the man and his son took the donkey to the market.

_____

_____

_____

As they walked along the <u>road</u>, a <u>man</u> saw them and laughed. He <u>said</u>, "Why don't you ride on your donkey instead?" "You're right!" said the man and he got on the donkey.

_____

_____

_____

Soon, a <u>woman</u> saw them. She <u>said</u>, "You're big and strong and that <u>boy</u> is tired. He must ride on the donkey, not you!" "You're right!" said the <u>man</u>. So his son rode on the donkey instead.

_____

_____

_____

58

Then, a <u>farmer</u> saw them. "Heh! You've got a donkey but you are walking. That's silly!" "You're right!" said the man, so he got on the <u>donkey</u> too.

_____

_____

_____

Finally a <u>woman</u> saw them. "That's cruel! Poor donkey! You must carry the donkey instead!" "Yes, you're right!" said the <u>man</u>. So the man and his son got off the donkey. Just as they were going to carry it, the <u>donkey</u> ran away!

_____

_____

_____

_____

Descriptive Details

Look at the pictures. They tell only part of the story. Write a sentence for each picture. Then add details to your sentences to make your writing more interesting.

Story Title: _____

1. Sentence: _____

    _____

    Sentence with details:

    _____

    _____

    _____

    _____

2. Sentence: _____

    _____

    Sentence with details:

    _____

    _____

    _____

    _____

3. Sentence: _____

    _____

    Sentence with details:

    _____

    _____

    _____

4. Sentence: _____

    _____

    Sentence with details:

    _____

    _____

    _____

Descriptive Adjectives

Note	Adjectives give more information about the objects you are writing about.

Under each adjective, list four words that are more exciting and have the same or almost the same meaning.

big

1. _____
2. _____
3. _____
4. _____

cold

1. _____
2. _____
3. _____
4. _____

hard

1. _____
2. _____
3. _____
4. _____

pretty

1. _____
2. _____
3. _____
4. _____

loud

1. _____
2. _____
3. _____
4. _____

ugly

1. _____
2. _____
3. _____
4. _____

scary

1. _____
2. _____
3. _____
4. _____

happy

1. _____
2. _____
3. _____
4. _____

Replace the words in bold with more exciting descriptive adjectives. You can alter the sentence if you wish.

1. Our principal was astounded by our **good** scores on the state tests.

    _____

2. Fido barked nervously when he heard a **loud** noise outside the door.

    _____

3. Tommy stared at the **big**, **scary** monster with **ugly** teeth.

    _____

4. All of us think that Mrs Blake is a **nice** teacher.

    _____

5. When you play the trumpet, it sounds very **loud**.

    _____

6. I want to win a prize for the **ugliest** costume.

    _____

7. I was **happy** when my dad won the lottery.

    _____

8. Singing in public is **scary**.

    _____

Descriptive Adjectives

Rewrite the sentences by replacing the words in bold with more descriptive adjectives. Use a thesaurus to help you.

The Royal Family

1. The king put on his **expensive** clothes and **beautiful** cape.

_____

2. The **beautiful** queen was wearing her **expensive** jewelry.

_____

3. The eldest princess had a **bad** shock when the **naughty** elves hollered.

_____

4. The **pretty** princesses were running among the **nice** flowers.

_____

5. The **unusual** fairy godmother appeared from behind the **big** tree.

_____

6. The **good** prince set off to fight the **big** dragon.

_____

To parents   Ask your child to pick out a fantasy creature from any storybook and write three sentences about this creature using suitable adjectives.

64

Date: _____

Descriptive Adjectives

Look at the picture below. Write down some details you can see in the picture, using adjectives to describe them.

Setting:
Example: clear blue sky

_____

_____

_____

People:
Example: small eyes

_____

_____

_____

Objects:
Example: small narrow boat

_____

_____

_____

To parents | Choose a detail from each of the three sections above. Ask your child to write a sentence for each of the three details.

Using Before/After Clauses

Note	Before and after clauses are used to tell when something happens compared to another event or time.

Combine the sentences by using *before* or *after*. You may need to change some of the sentences.

What Comes Before and After?

1. John had breakfast at home. John went to school.

    (Before) _____

2. Thomas ran thrice round the field. Thomas felt tired.

    (After) _____

3. We should take cover. We get caught in the rain.

    (Before) _____

4. The rain stops. We will go to the beach.

    (After) _____

5. Check for traffic. Cross the road.

    (Before) _____

6. Marcy washes the clothes. Marcy hangs them out to dry.

    (After) _____

To parents	Look at the instructions in a manual. Ask your child to combine two consecutive steps in the instructions using 'before' or 'after'.

Using Before/After Clauses

Combine these steps of a shepherd's pie recipe using *before* or *after*. You may need to change some of the sentences.

A Shepherd's Pie Recipe

1. Peel and chop the potatoes. Boil the potatoes in salted water.

   (Before) _____

2. Melt butter in a frying pan. Cook chopped onions and carrots in butter until tender.

   (After) _____

3. Add ground beef. Add salt, pepper and Worcestershire sauce.

   (Before) _____

4. Add beef broth and cook the beef. Add corn or peas.

   (After) _____

5. Place the cooked beef in a baking dish. Cover with mashed potatoes.

   (Before) _____

6. Use a fork to make some designs on the pie. Bake the pie in an oven.

   (After) _____

To parents — Ask your child to pick out a favorite family recipe. Help your child combine steps in the recipe together using *before* or *after*.

Using Comparative Adjectives

Note	Comparative adjectives are used to compare two nouns or two groups of nouns.

Write sentences to compare the subject of each sentence with the person, object, or place in the brackets. Remember to use the word *than* in your sentence.

Example: William is young. (Edward)
 <u>Edward is younger than William.</u>

Making Comparisons

1. You can sprint fast. (Sue)

 _____

2. The strawberries are sweet. (mangoes)

 _____

3. This football player is popular. (hockey player)

 _____

4. This café serves tasty dishes. (restaurant)

 _____

5. Sally is intelligent. (Trudy)

 _____

6. Kerri is good at playing the piano. (Adam)

 _____

To parents	Ask your child to say which of her friends is taller, shorter, has bigger hands / feet. Ask her to compare them using the word 'than'.

Using Comparative Adjectives

Use the helping words given to write sentences that show comparisons.

Example: (Wendy, thin, Anne)
<u>Wendy is thinner than Anne.</u>

1. (stone, hard, egg)

   _____

2. (fox, quick, dog)

   _____

3. (these mangoes, fresh, those strawberries)

   _____

4. (bedroom, clean, living room)

   _____

5. (these Math sums, difficult, those Science questions)

   _____

6. (blue tulips, attractive, red roses)

   _____

7. (Samuel, careful, Andy)

   _____

8. (wisdom, great, gold)

   _____

To parents Ask your child to compare something with a friend. On a separate sheet of paper, ask her to write a comparative sentence about the comparison.

Using Superlative Adjectives

Read what the Quarrelsome Twins are saying to each other. Fill in suitable superlative adjectives.

The Quarrelsome Twins

Sindy: Look at my _____ (new) toy puppy. It looks just like a real

puppy! It has the _____ (soft) fur and the _____

(big) brown eyes.

Sandy: Really? I think my train set is better. It's got the _____

(loud) whistle you've ever heard. It goes on the _____ (exciting)

adventures you can imagine!

Sindy: Well, I think my toy puppy is the _____ (beautiful) thing in

the world. It is the _____ (pretty) and _____ (nice)

toy ever!

Mrs Lorna: Now, children. Stop quarrelling. The _____

(important) thing is that you share your toys with each other. Then you will be the

_____ (happy) children in our class.

To parents	Ask your child to write another set of conversation sentences where Sindy and Sandy are comparing their things again. Remind your child to use superlative adjectives.

Using Comparative and Superlative Adjectives

Write down the correct form of adjectives in the spaces.

Compare These!

1. Roger finds adventure stories _____ (interesting) than fantasy stories but he likes horror stories _____ (good) of all.

2. Of all the presents, the doll is the _____ (expensive) but I think my teddy bear is _____ (lovely) than the doll.

3. This armchair is _____ (comfortable) than that one at Aunt Angie's but the sofa at Granny Wilson's is the _____ (inviting).

4. Ingrid is _____ (hardworking) than Tony but who is the _____ (busy) among our six project group members?

5. Although Frank runs _____ (fast) than Joe, Joe must be the _____ (thin) boy in our athletics team!

6. Uncle Eric has _____ (little) hair than Uncle Tom, but Uncle Richard has the _____ (little) hair of all.

7. The weather today is _____ (bad) than yesterday but it was the _____ (bad) last summer!

8. Mrs Williamson is _____ (strict) than Mr Jenkins but she is the _____ (friendly) teacher in Greenville Elementary School.

To parents Ask your child to write three more sentences using comparative and superlative adjectives.

Mapping a Story: The Setting

Note	The **setting** of a story tells when or where it is happening.

Imagine that you are writing a story for each picture below. How will you describe the setting? Write a sentence describing each setting.

Once Upon a Time

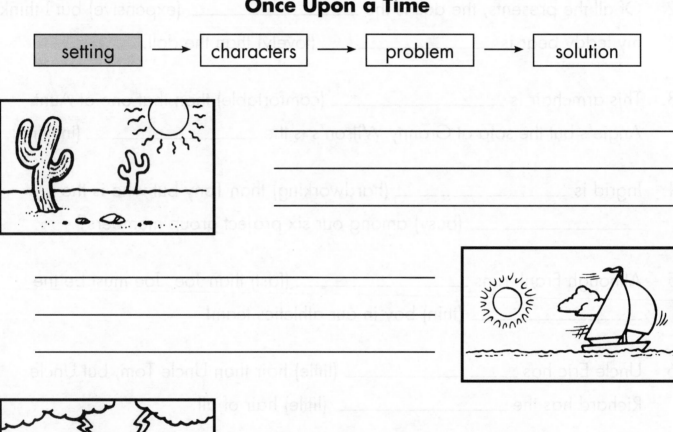

To parents   Ask your child to describe the setting of her favorite movie.

Mapping a Story: The Characters

Note	The people or animals in a story are called **characters**.

Some characters are likable and others are not. Write a describing sentence about each character. Be sure to give each character a name.

All Kinds of Characters

setting	→	characters	→	problem	→	solution

_____

_____

_____

_____

_____

_____

_____

_____

_____

Mapping a Story: The Problem

> **Note** To make a story exciting, one of the characters often runs into a **problem**.

Think about each character in the sentences below. What could happen that would make a problem for that character? Write the next sentence creating a problem.

That's a Problem!

setting → characters → problem → solution

1. Beauty Butterfly was enjoying the warm spring day.

_____

2. Jesse was supposed to wear shoes outside.

_____

3. Gabby could not wait to bite into her apple.

_____

4. Ben smacked the baseball into the air.

_____

5. Barney Bass had never seen such a big worm!

_____

> **To parents** Review the problems your child wrote. Ask your child why each of these situations would be a problem.

Mapping a Story: The Solution

| **Note** | At the end of a story, the problem is usually solved. This is called the **solution**. |

Read the beginning and middle parts of the stories below. Write an ending solution for each.

Good Solution!

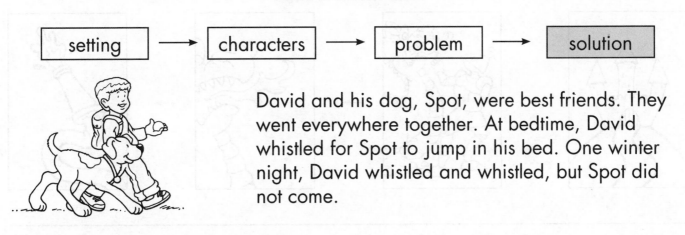

David and his dog, Spot, were best friends. They went everywhere together. At bedtime, David whistled for Spot to jump in his bed. One winter night, David whistled and whistled, but Spot did not come.

_____

_____

_____

Josh loved second grade, but he did not like recess. Josh's class was always the last one out to the playground. Every day, Josh ran to get a swing, but they were always taken.

_____

_____

_____

Writing a Story from a Map

| **Note** | A **story map** helps you plan the setting, characters, problem, and solution. |

Write a sentence about each part of the map to make a story.

The Mighty Knight

_____

_____

_____

_____

_____

_____

_____

_____

| **To parents** | Ask your child to replace the last picture with a drawing of her own. Then ask your child to write an alternative ending. |

Writing a Story from a Map

Note	Use a story map to help plan your story before you begin writing.

Complete the map. Then use it to write a story "fit for a king."

A Story Fit for a King

_____

_____

_____

_____

_____

_____

_____

_____

To parents	Turn the story into a puppet show! You can perform the puppet show together with your child.

Writing the Beginning, Middle, and End of a Story

Choose a story idea from the list. Then write a beginning, middle, and ending sentence to make a story of your own. Draw and color a picture to match each part.

An Original Story

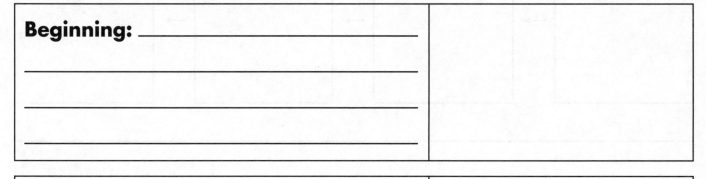

The Best Birthday Ever **King for a Day**
My Dog's Dream **The Magic Rock**

Beginning: _____
_____
_____

Middle: _____
_____
_____

Ending: _____
_____
_____

To parents Photocopy this page. Cut out the different sections and staple the pieces together to make a book. Your child can read the story to you.

Completing a Sequenced Paragraph

| **Note** | Sentences can be written in order of beginning (B), middle (M) and ending (E) to make a paragraph. |

Write a middle and ending sentence to complete each paragraph.

Under the Big Top

B   The circus started with a roll of drums and flashing lights.

M   Next, _____

E   Last, _____

B   The tightrope walker stepped into the spotlight.

M   Next, _____

E   Last, _____

B   The lion tamer came on stage.

M   Next, _____

E   Last, _____

B   The dancing ponies appeared in the center ring.

M   Next, _____

E   Last, _____

| **To parents** | Ask your child to think of one more kind of performance in a circus and add another paragraph to the ones above. |

Date: _____

Completing a Sequenced Paragraph

Write a beginning, middle and ending sentence for
each situation to make continuous paragraphs.
Use the words in brackets to help you write the
beginning sentences.

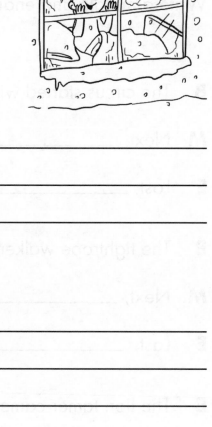

Fun in the Snow

(Paul, woke, snowing)

B _____

M _____

E _____

(sledding, friends)

B _____

M _____

E _____

(warm, house, dinner)

B _____

M _____

E _____

To parents   Revisit the paragraphs written above. Ask your child to add details to make each paragraph more
interesting.

Building a Paragraph: Following a Topic

Note	A **paragraph** is a group of sentences that tells about one idea, called the **topic**.

Imagine that you are planning to write a paragraph about each topic below. Write three ideas for each topic. The first topic has been done for you.

Terrific Topics

Gardening	Fish	Homework
1. flowers	1.	1.
2. vegetables	2.	2.
3. pesky insects	3.	3.
Sports	**Friends**	**Favorite books**
1.	1.	1.
2.	2.	2.
3.	3.	3.
Favorite movies	**History**	**Healthy foods**
1.	1.	1.
2.	2.	2.
3.	3.	3.

To parents	Ask your child to write three ideas for the topic "School".

Building a Paragraph: Following a Topic Sentence

Note	The sentence that tells the topic of a paragraph is called the **topic sentence**.

Draw a line through the sentence that does not belong with the topic.

It Just Doesn't Belong!

Topic: Dogs make great family pets.

Dogs have great hearing, which helps them protect a family from danger.

Most dogs welcome their owners with wagging tails.

My favorite kind of dog is a boxer.

Many dogs are willing to play with children in a safe manner.

Topic: The history of the American flag is quite interesting.

The first American flag had no stars at all.

Not much is known about the history of Chinese flags.

Historians cannot prove that Betsy Ross really made the first American flag.

The American flag has changed 27 times.

Topic: Hurricanes are called by different names depending on where they occur.

Hurricanes have strong, powerful winds.

In the Philippines, hurricanes are called baguios.

Hurricanes are called typhoons in the Far East.

Australian people use the name willy-willies to describe hurricanes.

To parents	Together with your child, read a paragraph from a favorite chapter book. Ask your child to read the topic sentence.

Building a Paragraph: Writing a Topic Sentence

| **Note** | A topic sentence is sometimes called the **main idea**. |

Read the groups of sentences. Then write a topic sentence that tells the main idea of the paragraph.

Missing Topics

_____

_____

One reason is that guinea pigs do not usually bite. Second, guinea pigs don't make as much noise as other rodents might during the night. Last, they are large enough that they can be found if they ever get lost in a house.

_____

_____

First, spread peanut butter on two pieces of bread. Next, cut a banana into slices and lay them on top of the peanut butter. Then close the two pieces of bread into a sandwich. Last, eat up!

_____

_____

Frogs usually have longer legs and wetter skin than toads do. Many frogs live near a water source of some kind while toads prefer a damp, muddy environment. Frog eggs and toad eggs are different in shape.

| **To parents** | On another piece of paper, ask your child to make a list of three subjects she knows a lot about and write a possible topic sentence for each of the subjects. |

Building a Paragraph: Writing a Topic Sentence

Note	Writing a topic sentence takes thought because your entire paragraph must follow the main idea.

Try These Topics

Write a topic sentence for each subject.

1. My Chores

   _____

2. The Best Book Ever

   _____

3. My Favorite After-School Activity

   _____

4. Appropriate TV Shows for Kids

   _____

5. Types of Coins

   _____

To parents Ask your child to pick one of the subjects above and write a second topic sentence for that subject.

Building a Paragraph: Writing a Closing Sentence

Note | The last sentence in a paragraph is called the **closing sentence**. It retells the topic sentence or main idea of a paragraph.

Closing Time!

Find a closing sentence from the box below to match each topic sentence. Write the closing sentence.

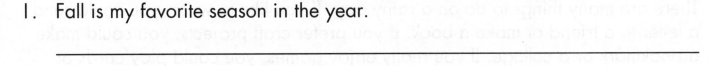

> Some gardeners in Florida and Texas can enjoy their flowers all year long.
> Of all the seasons, autumn is the best.
> Life would never be the same without computers.
> There are many subjects in school, but Math is the most difficult.
> Though dangerous, the job of an astronaut is exciting.

1. Fall is my favorite season in the year.

    _____

2. Astronauts have one of the most exciting and dangerous jobs.

    _____

3. Math is the toughest part of our school curriculum.

    _____

4. Many types of flowers grow year-round in the southern states.

    _____

5. Computer technology has changed many aspects of our lives.

    _____

To parents | Ask your child to choose a topic sentence from the previous page and write a closing sentence for the topic.

Building a Paragraph: Writing a Closing Sentence

Write a closing sentence for each paragraph.

That's All, Folks!

All cyclists should wear helmets while riding their bikes. Many injuries occur to the head in biking accidents. Helmets could help prevent the injuries. Helmets also make cyclists more easily noticed by car drivers.

_____

_____

There are many things to do on a rainy day. If you like to write, you could send a letter to a friend or make a book. If you prefer craft projects, you could make a bookmark or a collage. If you really enjoy games, you could play cards or build a puzzle.

_____

_____

The wheel must be one of the world's most important inventions. First, we would have no means of transportation if it were not for wheels. Second, we would not be able to enjoy many of our favorite pastimes, like in-line skating and riding a bike. Last, it would be very difficult to move heavy objects around without wheels.

_____

_____

To parents Review the closing sentences with your child. Help your child rephrase and improve the closing sentences.

Building a Paragraph: Following a Plan

Note	Follow these steps in planning a paragraph. 1. Choose a topic (main idea). 2. Brainstorm ideas about the topic. (You will need at least three.) 3. Write a topic sentence. 4. Write a closing sentence by retelling the topic sentence.

Follow this plan to write a paragraph about Ben Franklin.

Ben Franklin

1. Ben Franklin

2. a) inventor of bifocal eyeglasses and Franklin stove
    b) scientist who proved that lightning is electricity
    c) involved in writing the Declaration of Independence

3. Ben Franklin was a man of many talents.

4. Ben Franklin displayed his talents in many ways.

_____

_____

_____

_____

_____

_____

To parents	Read the paragraph with your child. Then ask your child to add a describing word to each supporting sentence.

Planning and Writing a Paragraph

Note	Use a paragraph plan before you begin writing.

It is time to plan and write your own paragraph. Use your own topic or one of the following topics: My Favorite Vacation, Collecting Coins, Our Pet Snake.

My Very Own Paragraph

1. Choose a topic. _____

2. Brainstorm three supporting ideas.

    a) _____

    b) _____

    c) _____

3. Write a topic sentence. _____

4. Write a closing sentence. _____

Use the plan to write your own paragraph.

_____

_____

_____

_____

_____

_____

To parents Challenge your child to choose another topic to plan and write another paragraph.

Planning and Writing a Narrative Paragraph

Note | A **narrative paragraph** tells a story. Its supporting sentences tell what happens at the beginning, middle and end.

Write a sentence about each part of the map. Then complete the plan for a narrative paragraph using the story map.

Do I have a story for you!

Beginning	Middle	End

setting and characters | problem | solution

_____ _____ _____

_____ _____ _____

_____ _____ _____

1. Write a topic sentence. _____

2. Write a supporting sentence for the beginning, middle and end.

    B) _____

    M) _____

    E) _____

3. Write a closing sentence. _____

To parents | On another piece of paper, ask your child to use the plan to write a narrative paragraph.

Planning and Writing a Narrative Paragraph

Draw pictures to complete the map. Then use it to complete the plan for a narrative paragraph.

Map It Out

Beginning		Middle		End
setting and characters	→	problem	→	solution

_____   _____   _____
_____   _____   _____
_____   _____   _____

1. Write a topic sentence. _____

    _____

2. Write a supporting sentence for the beginning, middle, and end.

    B) _____

    M) _____

    E) _____

3. Write a closing sentence. _____

    _____

To parents   On another piece of paper, ask your child to use the plan to write a narrative paragraph.

Planning a Letter: Main Topic

Note	When writing a friendly letter, find out the reason for writing the letter. Get the main topic of your letter after you have written down what you want to include in the letter.

For each question, write down what you want to include in each letter. Then decide what the main topic should be.

Reason: You are at a summer camp and are writing a letter to tell your mother about it.

What do you plan to tell your mother in the letter?

_____

_____

Topic: What is the main topic of your letter?

_____

_____

Reason: You have suddenly remembered a close friend who has moved away. Write a letter to him or her to get back in touch.

What do you plan to tell your friend in the letter?

_____

_____

Topic: What is the main topic of your letter?

_____

To parents	Ask your child to plan a letter to a friend. Ask her what she would write about and what the topic of the letter would be.

Planning a Letter: Elaborating on the Main Topic

Note	When writing a friendly letter, brainstorm for ideas from the main topic and organize similar ideas together.

You are writing a letter to a friend with whom you will be spending the summer vacation at his or her home.

Main Topic: Activities for the Summer Vacation

Here are some questions to help you brainstorm:

1. What kinds of activities can you do during the summer vacation?
2. What do you need to bring along to do them?

Write down all the summer vacation activities you can think of here:

Organize similar ideas together. Here are some suggestions:

1. Group activities together according to whether they are indoor or outdoor activities.
2. Group activities together according to the daily schedule.
3. Group activities according to what you like best and least.

Choose one of the ways above to organize your ideas.

Use the points you have listed on the previous page to help you write a letter to your friend.

_____
(date)

_____
(greeting)

Main Topic:

Write about each category that you listed on the previous page. Remember to group your points together.

_____

Writing a Friendly Letter

Note	A **friendly letter** has five parts: the date, greeting, body, closing and signature.

Use the five parts to write a letter to your pen pal.

Pen Pals

_____
(today's date)

_____,
(greeting)

(body)
_____

_____

_____

_____

_____

_____

_____

_____,
(closing)

_____
(your name)

Planning a Descriptive Paragraph about a Person

Note	You can describe a person by telling about how he or she looks. You can also tell about other information you know of this person.

Paste or draw a picture of your favorite family member, then fill in the correct details to answer the questions.

Personal Information:

Name: _____

What does he/she do? _____

Birthday: _____ Birthplace: _____

Family members: _____

Outer Appearance:

Look at the picture you pasted or drew and write what this person looks like. Start from the face and hair, then go on to the body and what this person wears.

_____

_____

Own Experiences:

Why do you like this person? _____

_____

Where do you usually see this person, and what would he or she be doing?

_____

_____

Planning a Descriptive Paragraph about a Person

Paste or draw a picture of your favorite famous person, then fill in the correct details to answer the questions.

Personal Information:

Name: _____

What does he/she do? _____

Birthday: _____ Birthplace: _____

Family members: _____

Outer Appearance:

Look at the picture you pasted or drew and write what this person looks like. Start from the face and hair, then go on to the body and what this person wears.

_____

_____

Own Experiences:

Why do you like this person? _____

_____

Where do you usually see this person, and what would he or she be doing?

_____

_____

To parents Ask your child to choose one of the persons described on this and the previous page and find out more information about him or her. Add on to the information your child already has.

Writing a Descriptive Paragraph about a Person

Note	Keeping a mental picture of the person you are writing about gives you a better idea of the right describing words to use.
	Organize your points according to the person's personal information, outer appearance and your experiences with the person.

Choose one of the people you have researched in the previous activities. Write out your paragraph by organising your information in this order: Personal Information, Outer Appearance, Own Experiences. Remember to use suitable describing words to make your sentences more interesting.

_____

_____

_____

_____

_____

_____

_____

_____

_____

_____

_____

To parents	Ask your child to find out more information about this person. Ask her to add on to the paragraph here, using a separate sheet of paper if necessary.

Planning a Descriptive Paragraph about a Place

| **Note** | You can describe a place by telling about its location and landscape. You can write about the physical appearances of the natural and architectural parts of the place. |

Paste or draw a picture of a place you have visited, then fill in the correct details to answer the questions.

Location:

Where is this place? _____

How do you get there? _____

Natural Appearance: (e.g. trees, parks, lakes, sea)

What does the natural environment look like?

_____

_____

_____

Architectural Appearance: (e.g. buildings, monuments)

What buildings and structures do you see? What do they look like?

_____

_____

_____

| **To parents** | Ask your child to do further research on this place and add on to the information here. |

Planning a Descriptive Paragraph about a Place

Imagine that you could create your own town. Draw out this town in the space below. Then answer the questions about the town.

Hitting the Town!

Location:

Where is this place? _____

How do you get there? _____

Natural Appearance: (e.g. trees, parks, lakes, sea)

What does the natural environment look like?

_____

_____

_____

Architectural Appearance: (e.g. buildings, monuments)

What buildings and structures do you see? What do they look like?

_____

_____

_____

To parents | Help your child improve on the details here by brainstorming more describing words to improve the descriptions.

Writing a Descriptive Paragraph about a Place

Note	Keeping a mental picture of the place you are writing about gives you a better idea of the right describing words to use. You can organize your information according to natural or architectural details.

Choose one of the places you described in the previous activities. Write out your paragraph sentences using suitable describing words to make your sentences more interesting.

_____

_____

_____

_____

_____

_____

_____

_____

_____

_____

_____

_____

_____

_____

To parents	Ask your child to come up with additional points and write a new paragraph using the new information about the place.

Planning a Descriptive Paragraph about an Event

Note	When telling about an event, it is important to include details about where and when it took place, and what it was about. You should also tell about the activities that happened in chronological order, from the earliest to the latest.

Recall a recent celebration you attended. Write down the details here:

Name of celebration: _____

Where did this celebration take place? _____

When did this celebration take place? _____

What kind of celebration was it? _____

For whom was this celebration held? _____

List down the activities at the celebration, starting from the earliest. Describe how you felt while they were happening.

_____

_____

_____

_____

_____

_____

_____

_____

Planning a Descriptive Paragraph about an Event

You are a reporter tasked with writing a short report on a special school event. Recall an exciting event you participated in or watched at your school and write down the details here.

Name of school event: _____

Where did this event take place? _____

When did this event take place? _____

What kind of event was it? _____

Why was this event held? _____

List down the activities that happened at the event, starting from the earliest. Describe how you felt while they were happening.

_____

_____

_____

_____

_____

_____

_____

_____

To parents   Ask your child other questions about the events she has written about. Get her to write down additional information about the events.

Writing a Descriptive Paragraph about an Event

Note	Remembering the scenes of the activities at an event gives you better ideas of describing words to use. Focus on things that happened and people's reactions to make your writing better.

Now that you have the details of your school event, you can write your report. Remember to use describing words and exciting verbs to make your writing more interesting.

_____

_____

_____

_____

_____

_____

_____

_____

_____

_____

_____

_____

_____

To parents	Ask your child to think of what people might say during the event. Ask her to include some comments using quotation marks.

Proofreading

> **Note** After you write a sentence, go back and look for mistakes. This is called **proofreading** your work.

Use the proofreading marks to correct the two mistakes in each sentence.

Out of This World

m̲a̲r̲s̲ = Make a capital letter.   (?) = Add a question mark.   (!) = Add an exclamation point.

(·) = Add a period.   (,) = Add a comma.   ☐ = Add a word. (Write a describing word in the box.)

1. Sometimes I can see mars Jupiter and Saturn with my telescope.

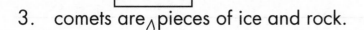

2. There are ∧ stars in our galaxy

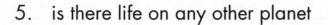

3. comets are ∧ pieces of ice and rock.

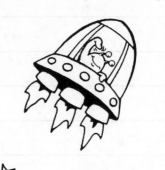

4. The sun is really a ∧ star

5. is there life on any other planet

6. Look at that ∧ shooting star

7. can you imagine traveling in space

8. i think I saw a ∧ alien.

> **To parents** On another sheet of paper, write two sentences about space with two mistakes in each. Ask your child to proofread your sentences. Is she correct?

Proofreading

Matthew's science report has nine mistakes. Use proofreading marks to correct his work. Then rewrite the report.

Smart About Saturn

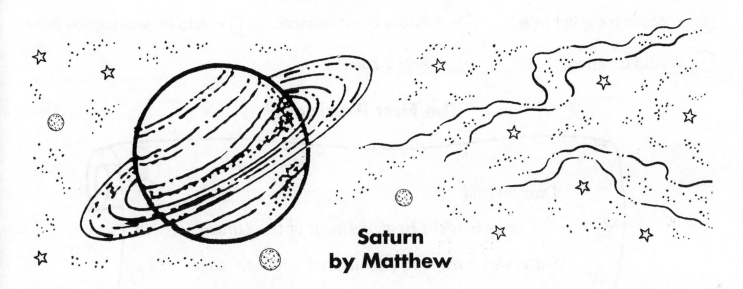

**Saturn
by Matthew**

Saturn is famous for the rings that surround it? its rings are made of ice, rock and dirt. The rings circle around the planet! Saturn is made of gas? saturn's gases are lighter than water That means Saturn would float if you put it into a tub of water Saturn has at least 17 moons

_____

_____

_____

_____

_____

_____

To parents   On another sheet of paper, ask your child to write a short report about her favorite planet and to proofread the report.

Proofreading

Note	After you finish writing, go back and look for mistakes.

Use the proofreading marks to correct eight mistakes in the letter.

<u>mars</u> = Make a capital letter.   ? = Add a question mark.   ! = Add an exclamation point.

· = Add a period.   , = Add a comma.

The First President

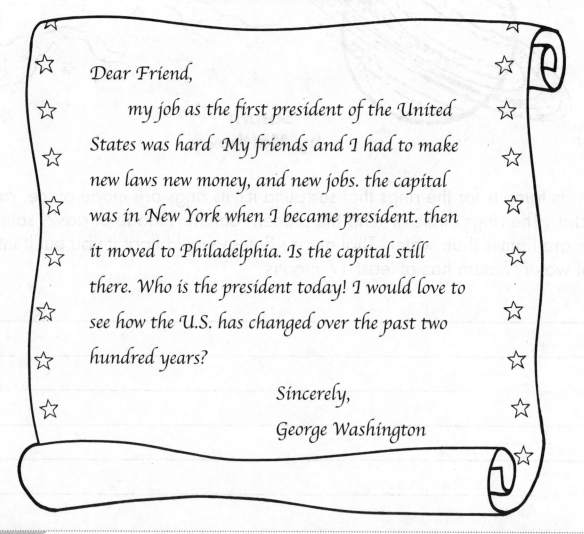

Dear Friend,

   my job as the first president of the United States was hard My friends and I had to make new laws new money, and new jobs. the capital was in New York when I became president. then it moved to Philadelphia. Is the capital still there. Who is the president today! I would love to see how the U.S. has changed over the past two hundred years?

             Sincerely,

             George Washington

To parents	Read the letter out loud with your child. Point out the moments at which there is a pause as one sentence ends and another starts.

Proofreading

Use these proofreading marks to correct eight mistakes in the letter.

<u>mars</u> = Make a capital letter.   ? = Add a question mark.

· = Add a period.   ! = Add an exclamation point.

Snow Day

the kids at Elm School had been waiting for a snowstorm? they knew school would be canceled if the storm brought a lot of snow last week their wish came true it snowed 12 inches school was canceled, and the kids spent the day sledding, building snowmen, and drinking hot chocolate. it was a great snow day

Find two sentences that had two mistakes and write them correctly.

1. _____

2. _____

Proofreading

Note	Capitalization and end punctuation help show where one sentence ends and the next one begins. Whenever you write, proofread to make sure each sentence begins with a capital letter and ends correctly.

Read the passage below. It is about an amazing animal, but it is not easy to read because the writer forgot to add end punctuation and to use capital letters at the beginning of sentences. Proofread the passage. Mark the letters that should be in capitals. Put the correct punctuation marks at the ends of the sentences. Then reread the passage.

Proofreading Pays

think about the fastest car you've ever seen in the Indianapolis 500 race that's

about how fast a peregrine falcon dives it actually reaches speeds up to

175 miles an hour how incredibly fast they are peregrine falcons are also very

powerful birds did you know that they can catch and kill their prey in the air

using their sharp claws what's really amazing is that peregrine falcons live in

both the country and in the city keep on the lookout if you're ever in New York

City believe it or not, it is home to a very large population of falcons

To parents	Ask your child to do some research and write a few sentences about the bee hummingbird, atlas moth or capybara. Then ask her to proofread the sentences.

Proofreading Sentences

Note	When proofreading, read the sentences slowly and carefully to look for mistakes in punctuation and spelling.

Correct the mistakes you find in the sentences. Rewrite them correctly in the spaces given.

Can You Spot The Errors?

1. "Its a great day to go swiming" said Jessie.

   _____

   _____

2. The boy's put they books pencils and lunchboxes into their schoolbags.

   _____

   _____

3. I cheked the room but their not there, said Mrs Stevens.

   _____

   _____

4. Whose the musician who has been performing since this morning.

   _____

   _____

5. There set lunches come with a choice of ice cream cheesecake or pie for desert.

   _____

   _____

To parents	Ask your child to write down three sentences with two or more errors in each. Correct the sentences and ask your child to mark them. Make sure that the sentences are correct.

Proofreading Sentences

Correct the mistakes you find in the sentences. Rewrite them correctly in the spaces given.

Can You Spot Some More Errors?

1. Kenny was sleep in the room when Jack returns.

    _____

    _____

2. Neither Lisa nor Sandy are interested in the prize.

    _____

    _____

3. Nancy gone to visit her aunt this morning.

    _____

    _____

4. The birthday cake, as well as the party snacks, are arriving shortly.

    _____

    _____

5. This book belong to he.

    _____

    _____

6. A large number of my classmates is coming.

    _____

    _____

To parents   Challenge your child to add in suitable describing words to make the above sentences more interesting.

Proofreading Paragraphs

Note	When proofreading a paragraph, read the sentences slowly and carefully, sentence by sentence. Make sure that the tenses in the paragraph are the same throughout.

Correct the mistakes you find in the paragraphs. Rewrite them correctly in the spaces given. Add describing words to make them more interesting.

My Father's Travel Collection

I love going up to the attick to look thorough my fathers souvenir collection. He keeps all his sourvenirs in a chet. My father travels very frequent when he was younger. His job as a pilot taken him around the world.

_____

_____

_____

_____

My father can remeber the places where he buy these souvenirs, and the people he met there. Some of my favorite item in the chest are the Russian nested doll the Mexican hat and the chinese ink painting.

_____

_____

_____

_____

Nowaday, my father still tell me stories about his travels. I enjoyed listening to his tails and always imagine what these countries look like When I grew up, I would like to travel round the world too.

_____

_____

_____

_____

_____

_____

_____

_____

_____

_____

To parents Write a short paragraph about another country, including at least five errors in it. Ask your child to find the mistakes and rewrite the paragraph.

Mini Writing Project 2

You are a reporter for your school magazine. Your chief editor has requested you to submit a short write-up on a topic of your choice. Plan and write your article, then proofread it before you hand it in to your chief editor.

Recap

When planning a paragraph, keep in mind a picture of what you want to write about.

When writing the paragraph, organize your information by grouping similar ideas together. Use describing words to make your sentences more interesting.

Proofread by checking for misspellings, missing words and punctuation.

1. Think of a topic you wish to write about.

Topic: _____

_____

2. Write down some information about the topic.

_____

_____

_____

_____

_____

_____

3. Organize your information. Write down the categories you can classify your information into.

_____

_____

4. Group your information and ideas according to the classification type you chose.

_____

_____

_____

5. Write your paragraph. Remember to use suitable describing words to make your writing more interesting to read.

_____

_____

_____

_____

6. Proofread your paragraph and correct the mistakes in your draft above.

7. Rewrite your paragraph correctly. Remember to include your amendments.

_____

_____

_____

_____

_____

To parents Ask your child to write the paragraph on another piece of paper and add photos to create an article.

Writing Tips

Writing Tip 1: Expand Simple Sentences by Using Adjectives, Adverbs and Prepositional Phrases.

Writing short sentences may be a good way to break up the flow of writing. They give readers a chance to pause. However, an essay cannot be made up of only short sentences. There are many ways of expanding your sentences. You can combine information by using connectors like *and*, *but*, *or* and so on. You can also expand sentences by:

- adding an adjective (a word that describes a noun)
- adding an adverb (a word that describes a verb)
- adding a prepositional phrase (a phrase that begins with a preposition, such as *on*, *under* and *by*, and tells where or when the action happened).

Compare the two paragraphs below:

Paragraph 1:

> The boy ran. His dog followed him. They ran down to the first floor. They ran to the garden. They played many rounds of fetch. The dog and the boy were tired.

Paragraph 2:

> The boy ran **quickly down the stairs**. His dog followed **close behind** him, **wagging his tail and barking excitedly**. They ran down to the first floor **and headed straight** to the garden. **After they had** played many rounds of fetch, **both** the dog and the boy were tired, **sweaty and smelly**.

By adding details to your writing, you can paint a more vivid picture of the scene for your reader. This would help to keep your reader engaged and interested in what would happen next.

Writing Tip 2: Make a Plan Before You Write an Essay.

It is always good to plan before you write. You can use a graphic organizer to help you plan your writing. A graphic organizer divides the main ideas or events in your writing. For instance, when writing a narrative essay or story, we usually begin with an introduction, followed by two to three events in a story, and then the conclusion. You can use the graphic organizer below to help you:

Characters: *Who are the main characters involved?*

Setting: *Where did the events take place?*

Problem: *What was the main problem that happened? What was the sequence of events that followed?*

Topic:

Resolution: *What happened in the end?*

Solution: *Was there a solution for the problem?*

Writing Tip 3: Write Introductions.

There are many ways to write introductions. Here are some examples:

1. Use a question.

   Have you ever heard of a mouse named Mickey? My favorite place to visit is Disney World.

   What is that thing glistening on the sidewalk? On my home yesterday, something shiny caught my eye. It was a diamond ring.

2. Use a quotation.

   "It's a small world after all!" Those famous words can be heard at my favorite place to visit. I love Disney World, and this essay will explain why it is so great.

   "Guess what I found on the sidewalk yesterday?" I said excitedly to my best friend Brenda. I told her about the diamond ring that I found.

3. Be straightforward and address the topic directly.

   My favorite place is Disney World in Florida. I love to go there to see all the exhibits, ride the rides, and watch the fireworks.

   On my way home from school yesterday, I found a shiny diamond ring on the sidewalk.

For all the above examples, the topics are the same, but the introductions are different. You can use a variety of ways to begin your essay.

Writing Tip 4: Write a Clear Topic Sentence and Support it With Details.

Very often, the topic sentence is the first sentence in the paragraph. The topic sentence gives the main idea of the paragraph. However, it should be followed by details that support it. These details are called supporting details.

1. After writing an introduction on why a person is your best friend, you may write a topic sentence like this:

    Jade is my best friend because she is always helpful to everyone.

    You should then give examples or details to explain your topic sentence.

    Jade loans people books and helps everyone with homework. She evens offers to help the teachers carry their books.

2. If you are writing a story, you might write a topic sentence like this:

    The troll was ugly!

    You should then give details, in the form of a description, to explain the topic sentence.

    He had long, black, greasy hair and a dirt-covered face. His teeth were green and slimy. He wore filthy clothes and was barefooted. He smelled like rotten eggs.

Answer Key

Page 6

1. The Sahara Desert is in Africa.
2. Do people live in the Sahara Desert?
3. The Sahara Desert is about the same size as the United States.
4. How high is the temperature in the Sahara Desert?
5. Once the temperature reached 138°F.

Page 7

1. The football team from Brooklyn School is here.
2. They are playing against our school this evening.
3. We are here at the stadium.
4. Are there any seats left at the grand stand?
5. Did you see the striker score a goal?
6. What an exciting game!

Page 8

One afternoon, Sue was walking towards her class. Just then she saw Milly whispering to James.

When they saw her, they stopped and went back to their seats. What was going on?

On the 1st of July as Sue was entering her classroom, she saw that all the windows were closed. When she opened the door, she heard a loud cheer. Milly and James had planned a surprise party for her!

Page 9

Answers may vary.
"Somebody turned out the lights!" exclaimed Joe.
"What makes you think I've been eating cookies?" asked Sam.
"My parents finally let me get my ears pierced," said Jenny.

Page 10

Larry picked up his skateboard and looked out the window. It was a bright and sunny day. "What a fine day for skateboarding," he said to himself happily.

He went downstairs. Mom was making breakfast. Mom asked, "What would you like for breakfast?" Larry thought for a while and said, "Pancakes, please!"

While he ate, Mom asked, "With whom will you be going skateboarding?" Larry said, "I'm going with Margie and Jensen."

Mom said, "Please be home by six o'clock for dinner." Larry said, "I will!"

Page 11

Accept all reasonable answers.

Page 12

1. Betty has two pencils, an eraser and a ruler in her pencil case.
2. Can I have a steak, a salad and a glass of juice?
3. Aunt Nancy has been to Arkansas, Colorado, Florida and Michigan.
4. My sporty brother enjoys football, basketball, volleyball and hockey.
5. The three colors on the American flag are white, red and blue.
6. Those trees are big, tall and shady.
7. My father, mother and elder sister are all at Uncle Jay's house.
8. I have Math, History and Geography homework today.

Page 13

It was sunset. The sky was a mixture of red, orange and purple. There were people strolling, jogging and running. Some had their pet dogs with them. I could see terriers, cocker spaniels, beagles and golden retrievers. Harry, Jack and Abby ran towards me. We love sunsets.

The deer is a beautiful animal. It can hear well, jump high, swim fast and see in the dark. In the United States, there are mule deer, white-tailed deer, reindeer, moose and elk. The mule deer lives in mountains, canyon lands, deserts and plains. The white-tailed deer feeds on leaves, nuts, berries and roots. The moose is the largest deer in the world. The elk is the second largest species in the country.

Page 14

1. D
2. B
3. F
4. E
5. A
6. C

Page 15

Accept all reasonable answers.
The following subjects should be circled: radio; sea; burger; sun; Mike; Michelle.

Page 16

Accept all reasonable answers.

Page 17

Accept all reasonable answers.

Page 18

1. My mother <u>loves</u> flowers.
2. Every day, she <u>waters</u> the flowers.
3. She also <u>puts</u> fertilizer.
4. She <u>pulls</u> out the weeds and <u>prunes</u> the plant.
5. The flowers <u>bloom</u> beautifully.
6. I <u>like</u> flowers too.
7. Sometimes, I <u>help</u> my mother with the flowers.
8. Sometimes, we <u>pluck</u> the flowers.
9. We <u>place</u> the flowers in a vase.
10. The room <u>looks</u> fresh when there <u>are</u> flowers.

Page 19

Jan was going to the zoo. She was very excited. Her mother packed a sandwich and a bottle of milk into her bag. Her mother said, "Listen to Miss Davis and do not run about." Jan replied, "Yes, mom. Can I go now?" Jan's mother smiled and waved as Jan skipped towards the school bus.

At the zoo, she saw many animals. There were the regal lions, the graceful giraffes and the playful monkeys. Soon it was time for lunch. Jan sat with her friends and unwrapped her sandwich. "Oh, it's my favorite cheese sandwich!" she exclaimed.

Page 20

<u>P</u> spoils the whole barrel
<u>S</u> every cloud
<u>P</u> catches the worm
<u>S</u> the early bird
<u>P</u> gathers no moss
<u>P</u> has a silver lining
<u>P</u> makes waste

<u>S</u> one rotten apple
<u>S</u> a rolling stone
<u>S</u> haste

The order of the answers may vary.
1. One rotten apple spoils the whole barrel.
2. Every cloud has a silver lining.
3. The early bird catches the worm.
4. A rolling stone gathers no moss.
5. Haste makes waste.

Page 21

1. There are three types of rocks on our planet.
2. It is more than 2000°F.
3. They are formed inside the earth.
4. Marble is a metamorphic rock.
5. Fossils are found in sedimentary rock.

Page 22

1. The name of the circus is Barker and Barnes.
2. The circus will be visiting Kansas.
3. The circus will be performing between 19 May and 24 May.
4. The show times are 4:30 pm and 8:00 pm.

Page 23

1. The name of the sale is The Annual Mega Sports Sale.
2. There are over 500 deals.
3. The sale will start on 14 July 2012.
4. The sale will last for four days.

Page 24

Accept all reasonable answers.

Page 25

1. Why are they laughing?
2. Should I bring out the cake now?
3. Did Pat come to the party today?
4. When are his parents coming back?
5. Where are the glasses?
6. Can Ivan have some chocolate ice cream?
7. Will we be playing games?
8. What will we be playing?

Page 26

Answers may vary.
What were you doing when I called?
Who is coming for dinner tonight?
Will they be bringing their children along?
Is everything going fine?
What time should I be back home by?

Page 27

Accept all reasonable answers.

Page 28

Accept all reasonable answers.

Page 29

Accept all reasonable answers.

Page 30

Accept all reasonable answers.

Page 31

Accept all reasonable answers.

Page 32

1. Fill a cup with water and add some flower seeds.
2. This will soften the seeds because they are hard.
3. Fill a cup with dirt while the seeds soak in water.
4. Bury the seeds in the cup until the dirt covers them.
5. Add water to the plant but do not add too much.
6. Set the cup in the sun so the plant will grow.

Page 33

Accept all reasonable answers.

Page 34

Accept all reasonable answers.

Page 35

1. Rita keeps her toys in the cabinet so they would not get dirty.
2. I will meet Brenda at five in the evening.
3. They are going for dinner at the restaurant down the street.
4. Trey and Johnson are playing ball at the basketball court.
5. My family is going for a holiday in December.
6. It is a good time to go out to play because the weather is fine.
7. Aunt Kathy will be visiting us before/after her meeting.

Page 36

Answers may vary.

One afternoon Ali Baba, a woodcutter, saw forty thieves at a cave in the forest. The leader said, "Open Sesame!" and the mouth of the cave opened magically. The thieves went in quickly.

Ali Baba hid outside the cave entrance and peeped in so the thieves could not see him. He saw the thieves putting their beautiful treasures in the cave. He saw a lot of treasures on the floor.

Ali Baba told his brother about the amazing cave. His brother decided to visit the cave that night. In the night, he went out when everyone was asleep.

Page 37

1. We are eating out tonight because Mom worked late.
2. We are going to Joe's Fish Shack although I do not like fish.
3. Dad said I can play outside until it's time to leave.
4. We can play video games while we are waiting for our food.
5. We may stop by Ida's Ice Cream Shop after we leave the restaurant.

Page 38

1. Cook sugar and water in a saucepan until the sugar has melted.
2. After you stir in the chocolate chips, set it aside to cool for ten minutes.
3. While the chocolate mixture is cooling, pour the nuts in the mixture.
4. Place the mixture into the refrigerator because that will harden it quickly.
5. This recipe uses nuts although you can use dried fruits instead.

Page 39

1. The melting snow cone sat in the bright sun.
2. Many excited children ran toward the crashing ocean waves.
3. My new friends built a large sandcastle.
4. My younger brother grabbed his favorite beach toys.
5. Our playful dog tried to catch the flying beach balls.

Page 40

Accept all reasonable answers.

Page 41

Accept all reasonable answers.

Page 42

Answers may vary.

1. Oranges are sweet and juicy.
   Grapes are sweet and juicy.
   Oranges and grapes are sweet and juicy.
2. I learned about the history of basketball for homework.
   I read about the history of basketball for homework.
   I learned and read about the history of basketball for homework.

3. I like carrots more than broccoli or cauliflower.
   I like potatoes more than broccoli or cauliflower.
   I like carrots and potatoes more than broccoli or cauliflower.

Page 43
1. Rene likes to eat stewed tomatoes and mashed potatoes.
2. Audrey and Candace will go to Holland next month.
3. I prefer reading adventure stories and horror stories to biographies or non-fiction.
4. Our market sells delicious local and imported strawberries.
5. Alexander Graham Bell was a scientist and the inventor of the telephone.

Page 44
It was a warm and quiet afternoon. Marty the cat was lazing in the sun and feeling sleepy.

Suddenly, Marty saw a movement in the bushes and the flash of a furry tail. He sat up and pricked his ears.

In the bushes was a busy and hardworking squirrel. The squirrel was gathering acorns on the ground and in the trees.

When Marty walked over, the squirrel scampered up the tree and looked at Marty. Marty decided to leave the squirrel alone and walked away.

Page 45
Accept all reasonable answers.

Page 46
Answers may vary.
1. He put the cup of coffee down on the table.
2. The hunter walked silently in the jungle.
3. There are many ripe apples in the apple tree.
4. Mr Johnson bumped into his neighbor in the corner.
5. People flock to the malls during the Christmas season.
6. She was listening to the radio while she washed the dishes.
7. Please brush your teeth before you go to bed.
8. The seagulls were flying above the sea.

Page 47
Answers may vary.
Once there were four mice. Every day they would look for cheese <u>around their mouse hole</u>. They searched high and low, <u>on the table</u>, <u>under the chair</u> and <u>in the kitchen</u>.

One day, they found some cheese! It was wrapped up <u>in paper</u> and kept <u>in the refrigerator</u>.

Whenever they could, they would gather the bits that had dropped <u>on the floor</u>. Then, they would quickly scurry <u>across the room</u> back into their cozy home.

Page 48
Accept all reasonable answers.

Page 49
Accept all reasonable answers.

Page 50
Answers may vary.
run: dash, race, sprint, dart
eat: digest, gobble, nibble, chew
write: compose, scribble, record, note
make: produce, construct, form, manufacture
move: act, proceed, change, cause
speak: state, tell, say, express
hit: strike, bump, bang, knock
look: see, view, notice, observe

Page 51
Accept all reasonable answers.

Page 52
Answers may vary.
1. Mike fell from his bicycle and **sobbed** in pain.
2. Sarah was so hungry that she **gobbled** her lunch hurriedly.
3. As Peter **dashed** to the toilet, he **bumped** into his friend Jim.
4. Tania **unwrapped** her present and **squealed** when she saw a pretty dress.
5. I **sprang** out from behind the wall and my brother **screamed**.
6. The kitten **stared** at the ball of wool and tried to **catch** it with its paws.

Page 53
1. Janice was **strolling** in the park and **enjoying** the scenery.
2. Suddenly, she **noticed** someone **gazing** at her from the bench.
3. When she **approached** him, she **realized** that it was Jon, her childhood friend.
4. Jon **grinned** and they sat down to **chat** happily.

Page 54
Accept all reasonable answers.

Page 55

Accept all reasonable answers.

Page 56

Accept all reasonable answers.

Page 57

Accept all reasonable answers.

Page 58

Accept all reasonable answers.

Page 59

Accept all reasonable answers.

Pages 60–61

Answers may vary.

Story Title: Beauty and the Beast
1. Sentence: The beast saves a girl.
   Sentence with details: An ugly beast saves a pretty girl who is frightened of him.
2. Sentence: The beast is talking to the girl.
   Sentence with details: The beast and the girl soon become friends and spend a lot of time talking to each other.
3. Sentence: The girl says goodbye to the beast.
   Sentence with details: The girl sadly bids the beast farewell and returns home.
4. Sentence: The beast is thinking of the girl.
   Sentence with details: The beast feels very lonely and misses the girl. He thinks of her very often.

Page 62

Answers may vary.

big: huge, large, enormous, gigantic
cold: freezing, cool, chilly, icy
hard: stiff, tough, firm, solid
pretty: beautiful, charming, lovely, fair
loud: noisy, boisterous, booming, rowdy
ugly: gross, hideous, horrid, repulsive
scary: frightening, creepy, spooky, intimidating
happy: cheerful, joyful, pleased, glad

Page 63

Accept all reasonable answers.

Page 64

Answers may vary.
1. The king put on his lavish clothes and magnificent cape.
2. The charming queen was wearing her extravagant jewelry.

3. The eldest princess had a nasty shock when the mischievous elves hollered.
4. The fair princesses were running among the beautiful flowers.
5. The strange fairy godmother appeared from behind the huge tree.
6. The brave prince set off to fight the ferocious dragon.

Page 65

Accept all reasonable answers.

Page 66

1. John had breakfast at home before he went to school. / Before John went to school, he had breakfast at home.
2. After Thomas ran thrice round the field, he felt tired. / Thomas felt tired after he ran thrice round the field.
3. We should take cover before we get caught in the rain. / Before we get caught in the rain, we should take cover.
4. After the rain stops, we will go to the beach. / We will go to the beach after the rain stops.
5. Check for traffic before you cross the road. / Before you cross the road, check for traffic.
6. After Marcy washes the clothes, she hangs them out to dry. / Marcy hangs the clothes out to dry after she washes them.

Page 67

1. Peel and chop the potatoes before boiling them in salted water. / Before boiling the potatoes in salted water, peel and chop them.
2. After melting butter in a frying pan, cook chopped onions and carrots in butter until tender. / Cook chopped onions and carrots in butter until tender after melting butter in a frying pan.
3. Add ground beef before adding salt, pepper and Worcestershire sauce. / Before adding salt, pepper and Worcestershire sauce, add ground beef.
4. After adding beef broth and cooking the beef, add corn or peas. / Add corn or peas after adding beef broth and cooking the beef.
5. Place the cooked beef in a baking dish before covering with mashed potatoes. / Before covering the cooked beef with mashed potatoes, place it in a baking dish.
6. After using a fork to make some designs on the pie, bake it in an oven. / Bake the pie in an oven after using a fork to make some designs on it.

Page 68

1. Sue can sprint faster than you.
2. The mangoes are sweeter than the strawberries.
3. This hockey player is more popular than this football player.

123

4. This restaurant serves tastier dishes than this café.
5. Trudy is more intelligent than Sally.
6. Adam is better at playing the piano than Kerri.

Page 69
1. The stone is harder than the egg.
2. The fox is quicker than the dog.
3. These mangoes are fresher than those strawberries.
4. The bedroom is cleaner than the living room.
5. These Math sums are more difficult than those Science questions.
6. The blue tulips are more attractive than the red roses.
7. Samuel is more careful than Andy.
8. Wisdom is greater than gold.

Page 70
newest; softest; biggest
loudest; most exciting
most beautiful; prettiest; nicest
most important; happiest

Page 71
1. more interesting; best
2. most expensive; lovelier
3. more comfortable; most inviting
4. more hardworking; busiest
5. faster; thinnest
6. less; least
7. worse; worst
8. stricter; friendliest

Page 72
Accept all reasonable answers.

Page 73
Accept all reasonable answers.

Page 74
Accept all reasonable answers.

Page 75
Accept all reasonable answers.

Page 76
Accept all reasonable answers.

Page 77
Accept all reasonable answers.

Page 78
Accept all reasonable answers.

Page 79
Accept all reasonable answers.

Page 80
Accept all reasonable answers.

Page 81
Accept all reasonable answers.

Page 82
Sentences that do not belong:
My favorite kind of dog is a boxer.; Not much is known about the history of Chinese flags.; Hurricanes have strong, powerful winds.

Page 83
Answers may vary.
Guinea pigs make good pets.; It is easy to make a peanut butter and banana sandwich.; Frogs are different from toads.

Page 84
Accept all reasonable answers.

Page 85
1. Of all the seasons, autumn is the best.
2. Though dangerous, the job of an astronaut is exciting.
3. There are many subjects in school, but Math is the most difficult.
4. Some gardeners in Florida and Texas can enjoy their flowers all year long.
5. Life would never be the same without computers.

Page 86
Accept all reasonable answers.

Page 87
Accept all reasonable answers.

Page 88
Accept all reasonable answers.

Page 89
Accept all reasonable answers.

Page 90
Accept all reasonable answers.

Page 91
Accept all reasonable answers.

Page 92

Accept all reasonable answers.

Page 93

Accept all reasonable answers.

Page 94

Accept all reasonable answers.

Page 95

Accept all reasonable answers.

Page 96

Accept all reasonable answers.

Page 97

Accept all reasonable answers.

Page 98

Accept all reasonable answers.

Page 99

Accept all reasonable answers.

Page 100

Accept all reasonable answers.

Page 101

Accept all reasonable answers.

Page 102

Accept all reasonable answers.

Page 103

Accept all reasonable answers.

Page 104

Answers may vary.

1. Sometimes I can see Mars, Jupiter and Saturn with my telescope.
2. There are many stars in our galaxy.
3. Comets are large pieces of ice and rock.
4. The sun is really a huge star.
5. Is there life on any other planet?
6. Look at that beautiful shooting star!
7. Can you imagine traveling in space?
8. I think I saw a little alien.

Page 105

Saturn is famous for the rings that surround it. Its rings are made of ice, rock, and dirt. The rings circle around the planet. Saturn is made of gas. Saturn's gases are lighter than water. That means Saturn would float if you put it into a tub of water. Saturn has at least 17 moons.

Page 106

Dear Friend,

My job as the first president of the United States was hard. My friends and I had to make new laws, new money, and new jobs. The capital was in New York when I became president. Then it moved to Philadelphia. Is the capital still there? Who is the president today? I would love to see how the U.S. has changed over the past two hundred years!

Sincerely,
George Washington

Page 107

The kids at Elm School had been waiting for a snowstorm. They knew school would be canceled if the storm brought a lot of snow. Last week their wish came true. It snowed 12 inches! School was canceled, and the kids spent the day sledding, building snowmen, and drinking hot chocolate. It was a great snow day!
Students may correct any two of the sentences containing two mistakes.

Page 108

Think about the fastest car you've ever seen in the Indianapolis 500 race. That's about how fast a peregrine falcon dives. It actually reaches speeds up to 175 miles an hour. How incredibly fast they are! Peregrine falcons are also very powerful birds. Did you know that they can catch and kill their prey in the air using their sharp claws? What's really amazing is that peregrine falcons live in both the country and in the city. Keep on the lookout if you're ever in New York City. Believe it or not, it is home to a very large population of falcons.

Page 109

1. "**It's** a great day to go **swimming**," said Jessie.
2. The **boys** put **their** books, pencils and lunchboxes into their schoolbags.
3. "**I checked** the room but **they're** not there," said Mrs Stevens.
4. **Who's** the musician who has been performing since this morning**?**
5. **Their** set lunches come with a choice of ice cream, cheesecake or pie for **dessert**.

Page 110

1. Kenny was **sleeping** in the room when Jack **returned**.
2. Neither Lisa nor Sandy **is** interested in the prize.
3. Nancy **went** to visit her aunt this morning.
4. The birthday cake, as well as the party snacks, **is** arriving shortly.
5. This book **belongs** to **him**.
6. A large number of my classmates **are** coming.

Page 111

I love going up to the dusty **attic** to look **through** my **father's** large souvenir collection. He keeps all his **souvenirs** in a **chest**. My father travelled very **frequently** when he was younger. His job as a pilot **took** him around the world.

My father can **remember** the beautiful places where he visited and **bought** these memorable souvenirs, and the interesting people he met there. Some of my favorite **items** in the chest are the cute Russian nested doll, the colorful Mexican hat and the exquisite **Chinese** ink painting.

Page 112

Nowadays, my father still **tells** me exciting stories about his numerous travels. I **enjoy** listening to his exotic **tales** and always imagine what these countries look like. When I **grow** up, I would like to travel round the world too.

Page 113
Accept all reasonable answers.

Page 114
Accept all reasonable answers.

126